All Star Hockey Press,
5241 Viking Drive,
Edina, MN 55435

MW00779034

For information, address: All Star Hockey Press, 5241 Viking Drive, Edina, MN 55435.
First published 2023.
Manufactured in the United States.

Printed by Farm and Home Publishers in the USA.

FOREWORD.

This book is very valuable to every hockey player and hockey coach. It is an excellent, instructional guide for all hockey players and coaches in developing a great shot, especially for hockey players in bantam, midgets, high school, juniors, or college.

There is a fantastic step by step easy to understand breakdown of the mechanics of the hardest shot in all of hockey, the legendary shot of Reed Larson. I highly recommend this book to improve the shot for every hockey player.

The shot mechanics are then analyzed by the premiere expert of hockey training and conditioning, Dr. Jack Blatherwick, Ph.D, Kineseaology. Blatherwick also analyzes the conditioning that built a foundation of strength to power the shot.

Improve your team's shooting with this book!

One of the best books on shooting.

Coach Bob Motzko,
Head Coach, University of Minnesota Mens Hockey Team,
Coach of the Year-2022-2023-NCAA Div. 1,

THE SHOT.
8 STEP BREAKDOWN OF
THIS INCREDIBLE SLAP SHOT.

"No player had as hard and as heavy a shot". -—Larry Robinson, Hall of Fame defenseman, 6 Stanley Cups with the Canadiens, 20 NHL seasons as a player, and 10 seasons as a coach.

"According to Dr. Blatherwick these activities/exercises of Reed Larson's youth and the frequency and duration of Larson doing these activities could not have been more optimal in building a foundation and preparing him for his slap shot."

Mechanics of The Slap Shot of Reed Larson. – Hockey's Hardest Shot, one of the signature pieces of Reed Larson's hockey career.

This is it! The spectacular, incredible, gold standard, unparalleled, slap shot of Reed Larson. It was the hardest shot in Minnesota High School Hockey! It was the hardest shot in college hockey! It was the hardest shot in the NHL! It was the hardest shot in all of hockey!

There are many different shots in hockey such as

- Wrist shot;
- Snap shot;
- Drag shot;
- One-Timer shot;
- Backhand shot; and
- Slap shot.

A player should practice each of these shots and get good to great at all of these shots. All shots are good shots to take. It is when and where that determines the type of shot a player should use.

The shot highlighted here is the slap shot of Reed Larson. This is a hockey shot for speed for any player on a rush up ice on the fly, Mike Bossy, was one of the best in that situation; or for a shot from the point, or from the top of the circle that would usually be a defense player but could be a forward. This is not the shot to take in all circumstances. This is not a shot of a center, or winger in front of the net, the shot of a center off a faceoff, or the shot off a quick passing play. This is not the one-time shot, the quick shot off a pass. This is a harder shot for speed for any player on a rush up the ice on the fly such as done superbly by Bobby Hull and Guy Lafleur.

1

The mechanics of Reed Larson's spectacular, hardest shot in hockey is described below in 8 Steps. You can make your shot better, faster, harder, and heavier. You will have your own shot not Reed Larson's shot. You can take a few things from the mechanics of Reed Larson's shot to use or make part of your shot. You should experiment with these 8 steps of Reed Larson's shot to find out what works for you which may be a variation of your present shot or a whole new shot. The building blocks of your foundation of strength will be different than those of Reed Larson, yet you can learn from and take a few things from how Reed Larson built his foundation of strength, and you can take a few things from the advice of Dr. Jack Blatherwick, PhD, Kineseaology, a hockey guru of fitness and conditioning.

First, line up 10 pucks. The first 5 times taking this shot the player should slowly go from one step to the next, to walk through each of the 8 steps, in very slow motion. Then the next 5 times taking the shot the player can increase the speed of going through the steps. Then the next 5 times should be at full speed. Full speed means as quick as the player can. Full speed means with an **EXPLOSIVE FORCE, a SUPER, HIGH INTENSITY** to focus every ounce of energy and strength on the shot. It is as if the player is doing karate and with the force, focus, and intensity that a karate player brings their hand down and breaks the board. Then take a rest or a break between the series of shots and then do again another series.

Accuracy is at the top, it is very important, it is paramount, it is one of the most important things in shooting. Accuracy is paramount as you take more and more of the shots and go through a series, fine tune your accuracy, getting more and more accurate. What is your target? Be accurate to hit the corners of the net. Be accurate to hit the net. Where are you aiming with your shot? As you take each shot get more and more accurate with each shot. Then for 5 times slowly go through the corrected steps. Line up the pucks again. Then do the shot 10 times at the highest intensity with explosive speed. Then take a rest then do 10 more shots at the highest intensity with a brief pause between each shot.

8 STEPS FOR THE SLAP SHOT OF REED LARSON
Step 1). The Stick:

Larson says sticks are very important for shooting. He says he can tell looking at a hockey stick what kind of shot a player has. When Larson walks in a dressing room and looks at sticks he can tell who really likes to shoot the puck or who has put his time into developing his stick and shot.. The selection of a stick is very important. Reed Larson is similar to the violin virtuoso closely examining the details of a fine, Stradivarius violin for all of its qualities when Larson closely examines the details of a fine, hockey stick looking at every detail of the quality of the stick, the height of the toe of the blade, the twisting of the blade, the strength and straight edge bottom of the heel of the blade, the strength of the shaft, everything, every detail is important.

A). Blade – a heel curve and a twisting blade with the twist beginning at the heel of the blade and opening up at the toe of the blade. This twist or type of curve was made from a straight blade stick homemade by heating up the blade and then with a towel and a door frame making the twist/curve by pushing the blade against the door frame. The heel of the blade should be very strong. The toe of the blade should be "fat" or a taller from the bottom of the toe to the top of the toe. This gives more accuracy with the grip of the puck. This gives more control, speed, and power to the shot in the follow through when turning your wrists down or rolling your wrists so that you will be looking at the back of your hand. That action of turning or rolling your wrist has the puck moving from the heel of the stick to the toe and off the creates the "spin" and "carry" on the puck. This type of blade makes the puck stay flush and lower.

Blade of the Stick

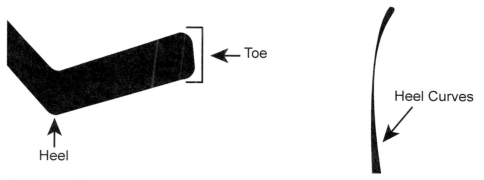

B). **Tape** – The blade should be taped the entire length of the blade from the end of the toe through the heel to where the blade meets the shaft. Cotton tape is best. Black tape should be used not white tape. It is harder for a goalie to see the puck coming off the blade of a hockey stick with black tape. Mario Lemieux and Guy Lafleur, two of the greatest scorers ever, taped their sticks the full length of the blade of the stick. When taping the blade do the overlap of the edge of the tape to face the heel and these tape ridges of the overlap makes for a good grip of the puck.

3

C). Lie of Stick.

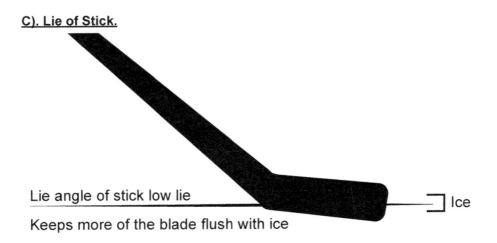

Lie angle of stick low lie _____ Ice

Keeps more of the blade flush with ice

Lie -angle of heel of blade and shaft – the lowest lie possible. It is important to have a low lie so that the blade is out from the player's body even with the body with the bottom of the blade flush or even with the ice. If the stick has a high lie not all of the bottom of the blade will be flush with the ice. **It is very important in the physics of the shot that the all of the length of the bottom of the blade be flush with the ice because this will produce much more force from the strength of the shot** than if only half or three-fourths of the blade is flush with the ice. A lower lie makes for a stronger, better, follow through which is particularly good on long shots. A low lie is better for defense, and a higher lie is better for stick handling in tight areas such as a center in tight and close to the goal roofing the puck and getting a shot up.

Another important part of a low lie with the stick further from the body is this allows for more muscles to be used in the shot and therefore more power; and this position allows for a stronger and greater whip swing transfer of wait that means more power.

D). Shaft of the stick – Always test shafts for stiffness, and weight. Based on the results Larson designates some sticks as practice sticks and other sticks as game sticks. A good stiff shaft builds in and gives "recoil" to a stronger degree that gives strength to the shot.

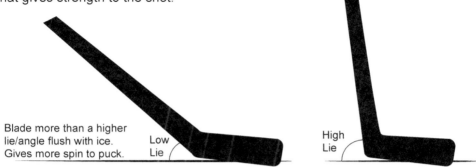

Blade more than a higher lie/angle flush with ice. Gives more spin to puck. **Low Lie**

High Lie

Hockey Stick:
- Low lie;
- Stiff shaft;
- Bottom of blade straight, not rounded;
- Heel of the blade not rounded, a straight edge;
- Heel of the blade strong;
- Toe of the blade good height and higher than the heel of the blade;
- Blade has a twist from heel twisting to open up at toe;
- Black cloth tape the entire blade from end of toe through heel with overlap of tap ridge facing the heel.

Step 2). Position of the body, stick, puck on the forehand side of body.

As discussed above with the low lie and the bottom of the blade of the stick the puck and the stick are out away from the body almost as far as a player can reach. This gives full, maximum use of the strength of the player in the upper body of shoulders, arms, and chest; and the full force of the transfer of weight of the swing, giving power to a whip action. If the puck is closer to the body it is as if the upper body muscles of shoulders, chest, and arms are restricted with a lot less power, and the transfer of weight and whip swing is substantially reduced and the whip is not given full strength.

The analogy to golf is the difference of the power of a tee shot with the golf ball teed up as far as possible from the player's body compared to a chip shot or 9 iron shot when the golf ball is close to the player's body and the upper body muscles are not in full force and the transfer of weight is less with a more limited swing.

Step 3). Motion-First Step of backswing: full swing and half swing.

Step 4). Transfer and Planting the front skate. Transfer of the full weight of your body from the back foot/skate to the front/skate (right shooter, right skate to left skate, and left shooter left skate to right skate). **The transfer is a huge part of the shot and is the swing of the shot. The transfer is combined with the planting of the front skate to STOP with the edge of the blade of the front skate 90* or perpendicular to the motion and body and turn the front skate in** towards the body with a right-handed shooter this to turn the front skate further

6

right and towards the body. See the diagram. The shooter with a good planting and stopping will probably have their body continue forward with a huge lean almost to fall forward. A strong planting of the front skate and turning in with stopping maximizes the power of the shot and without a good planting of the front skate the shot is much weaker.

Step 5). Contact-point of contact of blade of stick with ice in relation to the puck:

Transfer weight from from back foot to front foot.

All weight on back foot.   Transfer.   All weight on front foot.

The point of contact should be **18 inches to 20 inches from the puck on the ice.** As the player is beginning the swing down of the stick the back arm, right arm for right shooters, left arm for the left shooters should have the elbow locked into the swing, contact, and follow through.

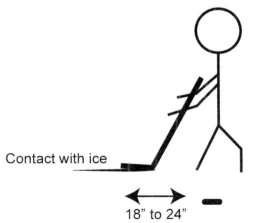

Contact with ice

18" to 24"

Contact with ice 18" to 24" before the puck

The point of contact should go into the ice a certain amount but not too much. There should be a small dent into the ice or a small divot in the ice if the blade is hitting the ice just right.

Step 6). The Contact of the stick with puck at heel of blade.

Contact with puck on heel of blade. Not on center or toe of the blade.

Step 7). Move puck down blade of stick from heel to end of blade as puck spins off the blade and follow through with shot. This spin gives the puck extra speed.

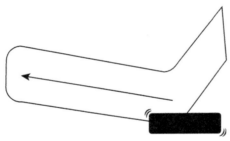

Move puck down blade, creating spin <u>at contact</u> with puck and <u>follow through.</u> This gives speed to the puck. Do this by <u>turning both wrists.</u>

<u>Right Shooter</u> - right to left
<u>Left Shooter</u> - left to right

Step 8). Follow through.

First, in doing Step 7 above with the puck beginning to move from the heel towards the toe of the blade turn or roll your wrist as the puck is moving from the heel of the blade to the toe of the blade. This turning of the wrist or roll of the wrist should be very quick and get faster and faster. When you complete this turning of the wrist you should see the back of your hand facing up. This turning of the wrist follow through gives the puck spin, and thus speed, power, and control. When you complete this turning/rolling of your wrists then get yourself back on both skates, weight distributed **in a good ready position,** ready to move forward, ready to move right or left, and ready to move backwards, then

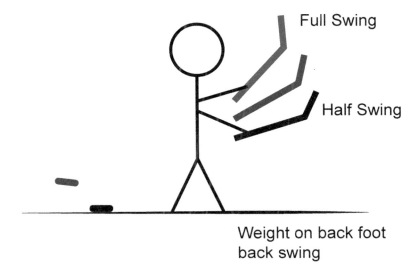

Full Swing

Half Swing

Weight on back foot
back swing

QUICKLY ASSESS the situation -Is there a rebound? WHERE is the puck? Is the puck coming towards you for a rebound shot? WHO HAS POSSESSION OF THE PUCK OR IS ABOUT TO TAKE POSSESSION, THEN GO.

   All of these 8 Steps and all of the parts of this slap shot make up the signature Reed Larson, no one else has these 8 parts in their slap shot. It is all Reed Larson combined with his ox strength and muscle/nerve memory of the shot that give it so much more power, it is all Reed Larson.
There are a number of players that use parts of the make-up of this shot such as use a low lie stick, use black tape on the full length of the blade, have a similar body position before taking the shot, yet there are very few if any players that use the following very unique features of the Reed Larson shot unique:

   • Blade of the hockey stick having a heel curve and a twist through the blade
   and the blade is higher at the toe than the heel;
   • Contact with the ice a good 18" to 20" before the puck (very few players
   contact the ice this far back from the puck);
   • Planting the front foot aggressively and turning it in (very few players do this
   as aggressively as Larson); and
   • Spinning of the puck. -Moving the puck from heel to toe on the follow

9

through of the shot and turning the wrist that moves the puck from the heel of blade to toe spinning of the puck;

PLAYERS DESCRIBE LARSON'S SPECITACULAR SLAP SHOT:
College hockey: From a teammate and an opposing goalie.

"I never saw anyone with a shot that hard, not even close."; describing Larson's shot in college hockey at the University of Minnesota. **"Larson had a cannon of a shot."**

Tom Vannelli, center, teammate. Captain and leading scorer of the 1976 NCAA Champion University of Minnesota hockey team with 26 goals, 43 assists and 69 points.[1] Vannelli won two NCAA Championships another in 1974 and played over 200 college hockey games about 100 games with Reed Larson as his teammate for 3 years. Vannelli played in the NCAA Finals game 3 years in a row winning the Championship 2 years. Vannelli had a brilliant high school coaching career of boys hockey as Head Coach for Cretin-Derham High for 3 years and then 15 years at St. Thomas Academy as Head Co-Coach with his brother, Greg Vannelli.

"First game I faced him in college, he shot from center ice and scored, beat me high".
Goalie, Eddie Mio, Colorado College, All-American goalie that season, 2 Time All-American, 2-Time All-WCHA, his Junior year and Larson's Freshman year, game of Colorado College and University of Minnesota at Williams Arena, University of Minnesota, on January 31, 1975. Mio played for 10 seasons in the WHA/NHL for the Racers, Oilers, Rangers, and Red Wings, WHA-44, NHL-192, total-236 games played.[2]
NHL: From 10 veteran players:

4 goalies,
2 defensemen,
3 forwards, and
1 God of Hockey:

Players who played against and with Larson, some who played in the NHL for 15 to 20 seasons and some who watched the NHL closely for 30 or more years.

*Goalie, Jim Rutherford.
"Larson had a tremendously hard shot, one of the hardest if not the hardest in the league."
"I cannot think of any player at that time that had a harder shot than Reed."
"I faced him every day in practice".
"His shot was so very hard because it was quick, so quick off his stick, quick off the release that would catch me, catch goalies, with its quickness in how quick and how hard it was." It was a shot that did not have a big windup."
Goalie, Jim Rutherford played goalie 15 seasons, 1970-1983, in the NHL with 457 games that included his first season, 1970-71 for the Red Wings of 29 games played and 2nd season for the Penguins, 1971-1972, 46 games played, both seasons facing the shot of Bobby Hull playing for the Blackhawks before Bobby Hull left the next season, 1972-73, for the WHA for the Jets. Rutherford became a very astute judge of skills, talent, and players as a veteran NHL player and then as an extraordinarily successful GM in junior hockey and in the NHL serving as General Manager for the Whalers, Hurricanes, and Penguin winning Stanley Cups with the Hurricanes in 2006, and Penguins in 2016 and 2017. He was inducted into the Hockey Hall of Fame in 2019.[3] He currently serves as the GM for the Canucks since December of 2021. Rutherford is considered one of the best judges of hockey skills and hockey talent.

*Goalie, Mike Palmateer.
"Larson had a really hard shot." "The shot was very hard, very heavy, the hardest in the league."
Goalie, Mike Palmateer, played 8 seasons, Maple Leafs and Capitals-356 games played, 149 wins, 138 losses, 52 ties,1976-77-1983-84. Larson's rookie season, 1977-78 Palmateer played in 58 games, 26-21-20.[4] Then post-career, a scout for 14 years for the Maple Leafs.

*Goalie, Mario Lessard.
"He had a really hard shot, a hard fast shot, as a goalie you could feel it."
Goalie, Mario Lessard, played for the Kings-6 seasons-240 games-20 playoff games,1978--84; 4 shutouts first season, All-Star-1981,[5] first 3 seasons the

11

same Division as Larson and Red Wings.

*Goalie, Eddie Mio.

"He had a very hard, very heavy, very fast shot".

"It was the most feared shot in the league".

Goalie, Eddie Mio, played 10 seasons, Racers, Oilers (1978-81), Rangers (1981-83), Red Wings (1983-86)-192 NHL games played, 44 WHA games played, 236 total, 41 NHL games played in the 1980-81 season with the Oilers[6] and Gretzky, Kuri, Messier, Anderson, Coffey, Lowe,. Player Agent for IMG for 16 years, presently Player Agent with Octane.

*Defenseman, Larry Robinson.

"It was as hard and as heavy a shot as any shot. It was an incredible shot that got everyone's attention in the league.

The shot was lethal. I remember talking to long time goalie, Mike Luit. and he told me he would have big, bruises on his body under his pads from facing Larson's shot, and no other player's shot would result in those types of bruises."

"What made Reed Larson's shot so great was its heaviness and the quickness of the shot, quickness in getting off the shot".

Larson, "did not have a big wind up or backswing ...the backswing was similar to Bobby Orr., short and quick, "

"No player had as hard and as heavy a shot."

Defenseman, Larry Robinson, played 20 seasons, Canadiens and Kings, Hockey Hall of Fame-1995, 10-Time All-Star, 6 Stanley Cups as a player for the Canadiens. considered one of the best defensemen ever, considered an offensive defenseman, Robinson was a leader of the Montreal Canadiens dynasty of the 1970's, most dominating team ever. 1 Stanley Cup as Head Coach of the Devils, and 3 as an Assistant Coach and Scout. Head Coach for 7 seasons with the Kings and Devils, and an Assistant Coach for 3 Seasons. For 35 years Robinson followed the NHL as close as anyone as a player and coach most of these years with one of the best teams playing.

*Defenseman, Kevin Lowe.

"Nobody shot the puck like that."

"Reed Larson's shot was lethal. Guys literally did not want to get in front of the shot." He would take his shot in many different situations. A very solid player."

"One of the hardest shots in the league if not the hardest."

Defenseman, Kevin Lowe, -played 19 seasons, Oilers and Rangers, 19 seasons, Hockey Hall of Famer, 7-Time All-Star, Hockey Hall of Fame, key part of the Oilers dynasty with the most offensive firepower of any team from the 1979-80 – for 13 seasons. 5 Stanley Cups with the Oiler; and 1 Stanley Cup with the Rangers.

*Center, Paul Woods.

Larson "had the hardest shot in the NHL". "It was a heavy shot, real heavy, it had great velocity."

Center, Paul Woods, played 7 seasons, Detroit Red Wings, 1977-1984, teammate of Larson from rookie season for 7 seasons. Detroit Red Wings Radio Color Analyst for over 35 years from 1989- present watching 82 games a year plus playoffs.

*Center, Dennis Hextall.

"Hardest shot in the league"

Center, Dennis Hextall, played 12 NHL seasons, 1968-1979: 689 games played, Rangers, Kings, Golden Seals, North Stars (5 seasons), Red Wings (4 seasons), 3-Time All Star, 3 seasons of 20 or more goals one season with 30 goals.[7]

*Left Wing, Nick Libett.

"He had the hardest and heaviest shot in the league. It was over 100 plus miles per hour... other players had shots with speed near or similar speed, but they were light, Larson's shot was heavy, when it hit you, it knocked you on your butt. No player had as hard and heavy a shot. His shot was always low, good to tip or deflect."

Left Wing, Nick Libett, played 14 NHL seasons, beginning with the 1967-68 season: 12 seasons with the
Red Wings and 2 seasons with the Penguins: 982 games played, 237 goals, 268 assists, and 505 points, 5 seasons with 20 or more goals, one season with 31 goals.[8]

*God of Hockey-"#9-Mr. Hockey", Right Wing, Gordie Howe.

"God, does that Larson have a shot..."[9]

Gordie Howe, The God of Hockey, "Mr. Hockey", The King of Hockey, no player played more games, and at the time of the end of his career no player owned more scoring records. Howe played 26 NHL seasons and 6 WHA seasons, for

33 seasons and a total with playoffs of 2,421 games played, Hall of Famer, 23 Time NHL All-Star; & 2 Time WHA All-Star. Howe played with Reed Larson as a teammate at the 1980 NHL All-Star game, played 1 season against Larson in NHL, 1979-80 season, and followed Larson's career following the Red Wings and following his Hall of Fame son, Mark Howe playing against Larson while Mark Howe played for 2 more years with the Whalers and then 7 years with the Flyers facing Larson.

From NHL-Newspaper Reports- from reporters following the Red Wings, Detroit Free Press newspaper.
"booming shot from the point", in the first month of his rookie season, game #6, October 1977.
"Reed Larson earned the first star for two booming goals from the point", second month of the rookie season;
"one of his deadly shots from the point";
"one of his booming shots from the point nearly tore the shoulder and head off Edwards (the goalie)"

Detroit Free Press- 1977-October, November-.

Within the first months of his rookie season, the newspaper reporters following the team described Larson's shot with these words in the Detroit Free Press. There were a number of times in the NHL when Reed took his shot from outside the blue line and scored, from 90 feet and at least one time from behind the center red line and scored. With these shots he simply beat the goalie straight on with this very hard shot.

REED LARSON'S BUILDING BLOCKS, THE FOUNDATION FOR HIS SLAP SHOT.

Training:

Water skiing.
Grandpa Ekblad, Ruth's father, purchased a small lake cabin when Larson was a young boy. The cabin had shoreline on Lake Pulaski in the City of Buffalo, Minnesota, about 43 miles west and a little north of the Larson family home in

south Minneapolis. It was purchased with the plan of an open family invitation that it would be a place for the whole family to use and the Larson family was all in. By the summer Larson turned 8 years old, the summer of 1964, a tradition was established, Larson's family, his brothers, and parents were there every weekend of the summer on Lake Pulaski at the cabin. Larson says each weekend, "we hardly left the water the whole weekend." Lake Pulaski was a medium sized lake, egg shaped, 770 acres, shallow along the shoreline with deep spots in the middle with a deepest spot of 87 feet deep,[10] clear water in general. It had cabins and homes along the shoreline packed in regular size to small lots with hardwood trees along the shoreline.

That summer of 1964 Larson began to waterski with Larson's father, Wes Larson, driving their 12' wooden boat with the green Johnson brand, 25 Horse-Power outboard motor. He pulled up Larson on two, wide, waterskies for Larson's first- time waterskiing. Larson was just out from the shoreline with his head and arms on the tow rope bar above the water with his ski tips above water and the rest of his body below the surface of the water. Wes gave the motor the gas full tilt and up was Larson skiing on top of the surface of the water. He was zipping along with great speed. What an exhilarating feeling. Larson hung on tight to the tow rope. He looked back at their cabin and the shoreline that was getting smaller and smaller. Wow, Larson loved it. Wes went out towards the middle of the lake and began a circle back to the shoreline at their dock. making a small circle swinging by the dock and shoreline. As he skied approaching the dock, he let go of the tow rope and skied without the tow about another 75 feet landing 40 feet before the dock and just out from the shoreline. Larson was hooked, hooked on waterskiing. His father swung the boat around coming up to Larson in the water close to shore and asked how Larson liked it and Larson asked his father he could go again.

It was a great duo, Larson and his father, waterskiing. He did go again after brother, Ross, had a turn and then his mother, and Larson was up on the skis again. Twice, waterskiing in the same day on his first day waterskiing. That summer on their family weekend trips to Lake Pulaski he would ski on Saturday taking his turn on the round usually in the morning and then again on a second round later that afternoon. Each time a small circle along the shore and back around to their dock. Then the same thing the next day on Sunday. Sometimes there would only be three or four skiers in a round that would take 15 to 20 minutes other times there would be four or five skiers and it would take an hour. Reed would ride with his father in the boat with another passenger as Wes drove

15

Reed, Age 8, on the dock at the family cabin at Lake Pulaski, a 42 minute drive from the Larson family home, summer of 1964. That summer he started waterskiing and the waterskiing regime began, waterskiing every weekend from Memorial Day weekend through Labor Day weekend, each day a round of waterskiing sometimes two or three rounds a day, age 8, age 9, age 10, age 11, age 12, age 13, age 14, and onward progressing to slalom, one ski, to barefoot in the summers of the late 1960's and early 1970's. A round of waterskiing went from 10 minutes those first couple of times waterskiing at age 8 to 20 to 30 minutes around the lake one round a day to two to three rounds a day, A regimen that built deep strength of upper shoulder, core, nerve memory, and reactionary strength.

Builds Deep Strength in:
Wrists, Forearms, Upper Arms - Biceps & Triceps, Shoulders, Upper Chest & Core

the boat for the water-skiers. Every weekend that summer they would ski and ski. They would usually have a morning round on the Saturday morning of the weekend even if it was a bit cold, or some waves on the lake. Sometimes the conditions were perfect, the water like glass, other times small to medium waves; sometimes a bright, hot sun, other times a light rain, the Larson family skied on, and on.

Water-skiing was a family tradition. Larson was getting better, and better skiing with jumping over the wake to his right then back over the wake to behind the boat between the wakes then to his left over the wake and back. Wes began to take his turns with Larson a little sharper that would swing Larson skiing way outside the wake and at greater speeds. It was fun, and there were sometimes that he would do three rounds of skiing in a day a round in the morning, a round after lunch and a round late afternoon or early evening. In his second and third summer, Larson's skiing advanced to have longer turns to have a ski route that was much bigger than a small circle going along the shore for some distance then circling back to their dock, a medium circle, that took more than 5 minutes sometimes approaching 10 minutes. Then later in the summer in the heat of late July and August, Larson's turn would be a big circle around the whole lake, a full ten-minute ride. Sometimes once a day, sometimes 3 times a day and the next day, Sunday more rounds.

Every summer weekend the waterskiing continued, usually a couple of rounds each day and after a few years the summer Larson turned 12 he started skiing on one ski or slalom skiing now behind a new family boat, a 17' Mariner Fiberglass with a 75 HP Johnson brand, outboard motor, driven by his father, Wes, a boat with a lot more power and speed, a great ski boat. Slalom skiing involved working many more muscle groups from shoulders down through core or torso muscles to upper thigh and quad muscles with all that was involved with more of a balance on the one ski, and more movement further to one side and then the other side balancing to the far right outside the wake and then outside of the left wake. Now at age 12, and going forward ages 13, and 14 and thereafter Larson's round was a trip around the lake paralleling the shoreline for a full circle of the lake for the 10 to 15 minutes a round. A new boat, even more powerful boat, a 17.5' Larson Fiberglass, with an Inboard/Outboard, I/O, 120 HP took over for an even greater level of skill for slalom skiing and more of a tension for working all of the muscles involved. The same routine of the same rounds on Saturday and Sunday every summer weekend, and then replaced by another upgrade in boats to a 16' Glasstron Fiberglass, 140 HP Mercury brand, with more power and speed.

Larson began skiing barefoot during the summer he turned 16 taking a round or two of barefoot skiing mixed in with rounds of slalom skiing. The barefoot skiing was a substantial increase in tension of the muscles especially the shoulder, chest, forearms and core muscles.

Gymnastics.

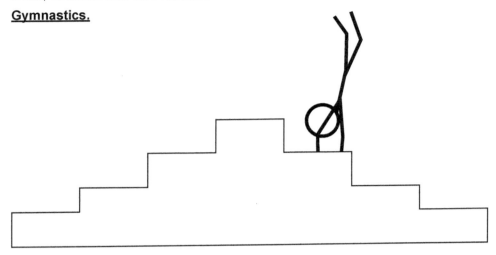

The same summer of 1964 when Reed turned 8, Larson began doing gymnastics exercises and classes through the YMCA at a summer, YMCA day camp, Camp Iduhapi, on Lake Independence in Maple Plain, Minnesota on the west edge of the Minneapolis/St. Paul metro area. Larson would go to Camp Iduhapi every summer for a number of years. In addition, Larson through the YMCA took gymnastics classes and was on a gymnastics team at Sibley Park that would go for 10 weeks. At Camp Iduhapi there were several counselors that would teach gymnastics exercises on gymnastics equipment at the camp. This equipment included a high bar, ladder, rings and a trampoline. Sibley Park also had gymnastic equipment that included equipment inside the Sibley Park Building and some equipment just outside the building. The equipment was as a jungle gym with a pull up bar and cross ladder, a dip bar, and a horizontal bar. The gymnastics classes were twice a week with a number of the routines and exercises being repeated several time each class. After the first couple of years Larson was becoming very proficient at the exercises at the team practices and at the camp. Larson began doing the exercises at Sibley Park on his own after practice. His parents built a high bar for Larson at the Lake Pulaski cabin. After several years of instruction, classes, and practices, the YMCA team from Sibley Park would compete at Gymnastic meets held at junior high schools or high schools. The first year was an introduction to a number of basic gymnastic exercises including rolls such as forward rolls, backward rolls, hand-stand, push-ups, sit-ups, and pull-ups. On the outdoor equipment, Larson and the class would climb up to the horizontal ladder and move along the ladder from one end to the other with their arms carrying the full weight of their body. Each summer through age 14, Larson took this class and became a member of the team. Each year the class progressed adding more repetitions and more sets to each exercise and adding new exercises. In the Park Building one of the new exercises was the head stand, holding his body up upside down by hands alone, moving several strides by his hands to a stair platform of 3 steps up to a platform and then 3 steps down.

When Larson was older at age 12 and 13 he attended a YMCA summer overnight camp in Wisconsin that had a number of gymnastic equipment to work and most importantly Larson's camp counselor had been a State Gymnastics Champion. This counselor worked with Larson each day for a couple of sessions each session up to an hour. The equipment included a trampoline that was part of the exercise routine. From age 8 to 14 Larson was involved with a number of gymnastic exercises as part of the team for 8 weeks, then with summer camp for 2 weeks, each summer, at his cabin beginning at age 10 each weekend of the summer, and in addition at Sibley Park on his own usually with the outdoor equipment in Spring through Fall, although many times inside the Sibley Park building.

Wrestling.

At the end of this same summer of 1964 when Larson turned 8 years old he signed up for and began a wrestling class and was part of a wrestling team at Sibley Park that met for 8 weeks during the Fall. Larson was also playing football on the Sibley Park football team yet the wrestling class and team met at a different time such as earlier on Saturday morning when football practice and games were Saturday afternoon and evenings. Larson was very involved with the wrestling season each year taking part in all of the practices and matches. The wrestling practices would have strength exercises of isometric exercises for different muscle groups including shoulders, arms, legs, and doing push-ups and pull ups. The practices would also practice moves against teammates with pulling and pushing against the other wrestler that would involve tension and building of muscle strength and tone, usually of the arms, shoulders, and chest. The practices and matches built up a deep muscle strength and power in his shoulders, arms, chest, and core. The matches were with other Minneapolis Park Board Parks such as Corcoran Park, Powderhorn Park, Longfellow Park, Kenny Park, and Lynnhurst Park. At the end of the year there was a city championship playoffs. In his junior high years his wrestling team would be from Folwell Junior High. Larson would end up having 7 strong wrestling seasons of Park Board wrestling. The wrestling culminated with Larson winning the City Championship at age 14 at the City Championship meet at Bryant Junior High School. Following that season at age 14 in 9th grade Larson no longer wrestled. The contribution of wrestling to Larson's muscular development and raw strength was especially a contributing factor with his beginning at the young ages at age 8, 9, 10, and 11.

Garage shooting pucks drill.

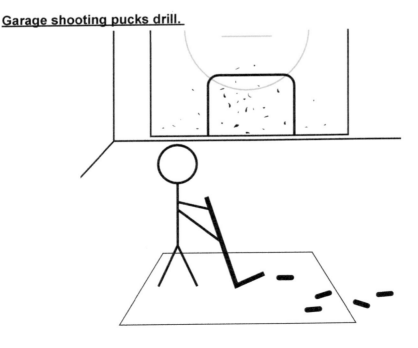

The Summer of 1968, at age 12, Larson and his father made a set up for a shooting pucks area in their garage at their home. As part of the work of Larson's father on occasion he would have a job for a couple of hours on a Saturday to clean out commercial spaces, sometimes a small, furniture store, or office. Larson and his older brother, Ross, would go along to help out. They found a wrestling mat that was being thrown out, and they brought it home and Larson's dad fastened it to a wall in the garage. They then drew on the mat the outline of a hockey goal. They then took a full sheet of plywood and fastened to it by glue a mini-boggan sled that was simply a flat sheet of hard plastic and put this down on the garage floor as the shooting platform. The platform made a shinney, slick, surface substantially equivalent to ice. Larson would take out to the garage some of his hockey sticks, his hockey gloves, and pucks, sometimes up to 10 pucks. The cars would get moved out of the garage and then the shooting platform would get set up facing the mat hanging from the wall with the outline of a goal.

Larson would use the mechanics of his shot as outlined above experimenting with sticks with different lies; sticks with more bend; heavier sticks; blades with a hook; blades that were of lower height and higher height; and straight blades. He would experiment with his stick blade hitting further back from the puck and closer to the puck. He would experiment with the pressure he would put on the shaft. Larson would experiment with the shifting of the weight of his body from his back, right foot, and all of his body, upper body and all to change and swing to his front, left foot, a planting of that foot. He would put all of his force behind his shot. He would put more and more energy and intensity into the shot. He would begin to have an explosive force in taking the shot, faster and faster with each shot. Larson would experiment with shots close to the ground and shots in the upper corner of the goal diagram on the wrestling mat. He would line up his pucks, 10 pucks and sometimes shoot in rapid fire one after the other, and other times he would pause between each shot and in slow motion go through the mechanics of the shot to work on a part of the shot. Sometimes he would do the shooting for an hour or more and other times simply for 15 minutes. He would do this shooting exercise or drill more and more often so he was doing it almost every day or some days a couple of times a day and then skip a day or two. Sometimes he would do it in the later evening when it was dark out. Normally he would do this garage shooting exercise by himself and a few times with a hockey teammate. Larson did not do the garage shooting in the winter it was not good to move the cars and mostly it was too cold in late fall or the winter yet in the Spring through early Fall it was Larson's regular routine.

During the school year Larson would do the shooting drill after getting home from school and later after supper sometimes doing it simply to get a break and out of the house. Each time working on this shot, his shot with its distinguishing characteristics. He was fine tuning the shot and also building the CNS-Central Nervous System-memory of muscles for each step of the shot. Taking the shot as fast as he could a number of times and repeating that. With all the repetitions his muscles supporting the shot were getting stronger and the shot was becoming harder and harder, faster and faster, more accurate and more accurate. Larson, the summer of age 12, 13, and 14, his last Pee Wee year and his Bantam years he continued and continued the garage shooting making it a regular, daily routine. Then in the winter months in the hockey season he transferred the shot to the ice. The garage shooting exercise continued through his high school years fine tuning more what he had begun to really develop on the ice with strong skating built on a foundation of Sibley Park ice so that the shot came while skating hard on a rush or as receiving a pass to shoot from the point.

The exercises, and the activities of waterskiing, gymnastics, and wrestling that Larson began at age 8 and continued through age 14 were fundamental in building muscle tone, deep strength and power for his upper body of upper shoulders, back shoulders, upper arms, forearms, and wrists, and of his core muscles, all key for use in his shot. In each of these activities there were many, many, repetitions. Waterskiing even at the beginning or the second year or two would be a trip around Lake Pulaski that was about 10 minutes. Then he would ski again when it was his turn about 45 minutes later and then go again, all in one Saturday afternoon. The next day, Sunday, he would do it again, possibly having a 4th time skiing that day. Then the next weekend the same thing on a Saturday and Sunday, every weekend of the summer, Memorial Day through Labor Day, about 12 weekends. Waterskiing worked primarily the arms and chest with Larson holding or pulling on the tow rope bar, a single bar or double bar, that was similar to the old, conventional, isometric exercises of pulling your arms in with resistance for a count to ten seconds then doing it three times. Larson water skiing was super isometrics for ten minutes of 60 seconds so 600 seconds instead of 30 seconds. With water skiing, there was motion from side-to-side skiing to the wake then outside the wake and back working the muscles to the side of the chest and the side of the arms. The pull of the boat on the tow rope was building muscle tone and strength, deep powerful strength.

The building blocks, the foundation or the forming and molding for the super hard shot of Reed Larson began and were especially strong between the ages

8 to 14 of: waterskiing, gymnastics, wrestling, and the garage shooting set up at age 12.

Anaylsis by Dr. Jack Blatherwick, Ph.D, Kinesiology, of Larson's Slap Shot & Exercises & Training

Coach Dr. Jack Blatherwick is the hockey conditioning guru par excellence of the hockey world. Dr. Jack Blatherwick was relied upon by the 1980 U.S. Olympic Hockey Coach Herb Brooks, relied on by NHL teams for years, relied upon and looked to by the hockey world.! He is the skating guru! He has worked with Coach Herb Brooks and worked for a long time for the NHL Washington Capitals and several other NHL teams, such as the New York Rangers, and New Jersey Devils as the conditioning and training consultant/advisor. Dr. Jack Blatherwick, PhD, Sports, Physiology, Kinesiology is recognized as the renowned hockey conditioning, hockey training expert, the skating whisperer beginning working with Coach Herb Brooks with the University of Minnesota hockey team in the late 1970's, 1980 U.S. Gold Medal Olympic Team, to working with NHL teams, Olympic teams, college teams, high school and youth teams for over 4 decades. Dr. Blatherwick has worked with many coaches at the NHL level, Olympics, college level, and high school level. He has served as Head Coach for Breck School in Minneapolis for 11 years and served as Head Hockey Coach for Minnehaha Academy, Wayzata High School, Hopkins High School, and Hamline University. He has visited the former Soviet Union to work with elite coaches and players. He is the author of numerous coaching seminar manuals, and articles. He has been a long-time columnist for "Let Play Hockey" magazine. He is the author of "Over-Speed Skill Training For Hockey" (USA Hockey, 1992). Dr. Blatherwick was inducted into the Minnesota High School Coaches Association Hall of Fame in 2009. He was awarded the Lester Patrick Award by the NHL and USA Hockey in 2019 for his huge contributions to promoting and supporting hockey in the U.S.[11]

According to Dr. Blatherwick these activities/exercises of Reed Larson's youth and the frequency and duration of Larson doing these activities could not have been more optimal in building a foundation and preparing him for his slap shot. It would not have been any more perfect or optimal if at age 8 Larson had a panel of 5 experts, highly paid exercise kinesiologists and hockey coaches to prescribe activities for him for the next six years in order to have one of the hardest slap shots of all time. Although Dr. Blatherwick points out there was not then and there still is very little or close to no science of understanding optimal exercises for skating and hockey skills such as a hockey slap shot. So, if at age 8 or 10 Larson had met with experts they would most probably not have been able to advise him at that time to do these exercises or any exercises from any base of knowledge. What Larson did was beyond any knowledge at the time at the highest levels of hockey, Larson was years ahead of the best training.

Blatherwick said, in addition to building upper body, arm, and wrist strength, these exercises built deep strength of core muscles that are a key part of the motion of the swing and turn of the body when taking a slap shot. That motion is similar to the swing involving the transfer of weight and strength in a golf swing or the swing or "turn" of a baseball pitcher in the throwing movement of pitching.

Blatherwick pointed out several other benefits.

One, was building reactive muscle strength especially water skiing with the tension of the tow rope while moving to the right and to the left to go outside the wake as Larson would do while skiing on two skis, then by age 11 and 12 skiing on one ski, or slalom ski, moving his body from far to one side then far to the other side and even older at age 16 when he would do barefoot skiing with even more pull, or more tension, or resistance on the tow rope.

Second, was **building muscle memory, more accurately CNS,** central nervous system memory and strength, deep, strong muscles with the many repetitions in each of these activities, the many times water skiing; the regular gymnastic classes, and meets; and the regular wrestling classes, practices and meets.

Third, was the building, of what Blatherwick and others call, **"athlete's strength"** strength built not from weight training but from many, many repetitions of the activity itself such as the "garage shooting pucks set up", and the many, many repetitions of the motions from these exercises that gave this deep "athlete's strength" to Larson.

Blatherwick primarily described as key importance the stretching, reflex muscles and reactive memory of muscles that came from these activities of Larson's youth. Dr. Blatherwick, states:

"The same basic movement in the hips that Reed makes when he shoots – the same as a tennis forehand, a quarterback when he passes, it initiates the rotation, and core muscles ensure that the upper body is rotating faster like a whip. [It is this deep strength through repetition that allows this 'whip' to be quicker, and stronger.] There is a lot of stretch reflex for each muscle group up the chain. That means for example the pectoral muscles of the chest are stretched by the rotation of the torso, which was itself stretched by the twisting motion from the hips. The stretch reflex is this: every muscle when stretched, contracts against that stretch. As a neuro-physiologist I say the learning of these complex but sub conscious reflexes must be learned at young ages. The repetitions of these exercises of Reed's youth might build some strength and endurance but their major value to a potential athlete is to require reactions to unknown obstacles or uncertain footing hundreds of times each minute: sprinting or skating on a rough surface with holes and cracks; pushing and pulling against a moving person – not pushing – pulling a barbell that move only in one plane. This is the essence of challenging the Central Nervous System, "CNS" during childhood and adolescence. That is the priority of young athletes. What happens to the heart, lungs, and muscles is a byproduct – NOT the first priority in planning the program. Reed's plan worked even though no one planned it."

In summary, Dr. Blatherwick's analysis is that all of these activities of Reed Larson at age 8 through 14, with their many repetitions and the garage shooting drill with numerous repetitions beginning at age 12, provided the building blocks of central nervous system strength and strength throughout the critical parts of the body for making Reed Larson's shot so very hard especially with the characteristics of these exercises of the reactionary nerve strength and memory.

For Dr. Blatherwick, another big part of the strength of Larson's shot is in the mechanics or physics of the shot with the huge transfer of weight and strength in his swing/shot to his front foot, his left foot in Step #4 above, also called the "whip transfer". Dr. Blatherwick watched Larson play in college hockey a number of times and watched him many times in the NHL as Blatherwick was working with a number of NHL teams through the 1980's. Blatherwick says Larson with his shot planted his front skate and turned it in. Larson did more of the planting and stopping of that front foot/skate than any other player Blatherwick ever saw. It was almost as if his left foot turned in and stopped or momentarily stopped for a second or two. Blatherwick has never seen any other player with these mechanics on a shot as Larson does it, with this aggressive planting of the forward foot. As a matter of the science of physics these mechanics results in using more of the force of the transfer of weight and strength to create more power, and more of the force of the "whip transfer" into the shot.

Blatherwick explains the importance of the "planting" and stopping of that front foot/skate with the analogy of the movements a shot putter as the shot putter moves across the shot-put circle platform to throw the shot. A shot putter who throws the shot, the weighted ball, while moving across the platform without an abrupt planting of their front foot and stopping, does not have anywhere near the force or resulting distance than a good technique of planting the front foot that transfers the weight transfer and power to the throw of the shot probably able to travel twice as far, a shot/throw of only 60 feet thrown while moving across the platform compared to a shot/throw of 120 feet with the planting of the front foot and stopping. Similarly, a hockey player taking a shot without the strong transfer of weight and even more without a planting the front foot/skate has a much weaker shot. Larson did not need to think about any of this because he had with these mechanics and with his huge repetitions of shooting all of these steps of his shot down deep in his nervous system memory and muscle strength. A muscle strength and nerve strength that gives everything extra quickness. His shot happens lightning fast in its mechanics, its quickness and in speed. It is explosive, all of which results in a very hard shot.

Hockey sticks.

Hockey sticks were very important to Larson in improving his shot. In his development he used many different brands of hockey sticks, sizes, lies, shafts, and blades. Larson started out in youth hockey using a Northland Custom Pro brand hockey stick. He continued using those sticks on occasion through youth hockey and in high school using a Victoriaville, Louisville, and Sherbrooke. Then in college Larson used a Christian Bros. brand stick and in the NHL a Koho brand laminated hockey stick.

Twisted curve blade.

Larson bought sticks with a slight curve in the blade and modified them by heating them up and putting his own twist curve on the blade. In youth hockey and high school hockey he would experiment with a number of different types of sticks to see if he could find one better than the stick he was using. He was always experimenting. In Bantam and high school years his shot was the hardest around, harder than anyone else. Larson felt he made his shot even better in college for a number of reasons including getting stronger and bigger and one of the chief reasons he attributes to improving his shot with even more speed and control was the quality of the sticks he used.

One of the benefits of being a member of the University of Minnesota hockey team was that he could "pattern" his stick exactly the way he wanted it to Christian Bros. hockey sticks. The team supplied him sticks from Christian Bros. with the "pattern" he wanted, and his name on it. Larson would give the details of the straight blade, the lie, and other dimensions using the Christian Bros. Jude Drouin model as his model with everything just how he wanted, and within a week or two he could not believe it he would get sticks that were near perfect to how he wanted them. They were his personal sticks. Larson "loved it" Larson called them "really good sticks, a little heavy". He was able to better shape the blade the way he wanted it compared to other hockey sticks. The blades were tougher and lasted longer than any blades he had used before. The shaft was much more consistent, a heavier shaft that gave a big bend, and a big whip, "a better recoil". Larson considered having these Christian Bros. hockey sticks " a vast improvement" in his shot that already was the best.

All of this combined to make the signature of Reed Larson his iconic slap shot. The slap shot combined with his other wonderful, strong skating, stick handling, defending, and team play that resulted in his All-Star recognition and his scoring records with his slap shot leading the way.

Reed Larson, #28, Red Wings, dominating player in the NHL for 12 Full Seasons: top of the NHL for 9 seasons: Rookie season-1977-78 – 1985-86, with the Red Wings, All-Star seasons and at the top or near the top in many Defense Records of Achievement such as #1 Defense Most Goals for the 9 seasons; #1 Defense Most Goals in a season, and many seasons in Top 5 Most Goals in a season in a period of a Golden Age of Offensive Defensemen. -#5 All-Time Defense Most Goals Per Game. Total 14 seasons in NHL-1977-1990-904 Games Played-222 goals-463 assists-685 points. Larson had the hardest shot in hockey.
[Public Doman-Ice Hockey Wiki]

#5 All-Time for Defensemen Most Goals Per Game.

#1 Bobby Orr;

#2 Denis Potvin;

#3 Paul Coffey;

#4 Ray Bourque;

#5 Reed Larson;

#6 Al McInnis;

#7 Doug Wilson;

#8 Phil Housley;

#9 Shea Weber;

#10 Mark Howe;

#11 Brian Leetch;

#12 Steve Duchesne;

Guy Lapointe;

Brad Park;

Al Ifrate;

Rob Blake;

Larry Murphy;

Nicklas Lidstrom;

John Carlson;

Larry Robinson

[Does not include players with less than 657 games played so for an 80 to 82 game season – at least 9 to 10 seasons, as 657 is the number of games played by Bobby Orr.

#5 All-Time for Defensemen Most Seasons of 20 or more goals with 6 seasons:

#1 - 9 Seasons ----Denis Potvin-------- 15 seasons played;

#1 - 9 Sesons------Ray Bourgue ------ 22 seasons played;

#2 - 7 Seasons ----Bobby Orr ---------- 9 seasons played;

#2 - 7 Seasons ----Phil Housley ------- 21 seasons played;

#2 - 7 Seasons ----Al Mcinnis ---------- 20 seasons played;

#3 - 6 Seasons ---Reed Larson ------ 12 seasons played;

#3 - 6 Seasons ----Paul Coffey --------- 21 seasons played

*25 or more games to a season.

"All other defensemen such as: Larry Murphy (5 seasons); Brad Park (3 seasons));

29

Bjore Salming (3 seasons); Doug Wilson (3 seasons); Gary Suter (3 seasons); Chris Chelios (1 season); Nicklas Lidstrom (1 season); and Larry Robinson (0 seasons).

#1 Most Goals by Defenseman over 9 Seasons -#1-Reed Larson-209;

9 seasons: 1977-78-1985-86--all players played all 9 seasons except Brad Park who played 8 seasons.

#1 --- **Reed Larson -------- 209 Goals.**

#2 --- *Mark Howe --------- 204 Goals (includes 2 WHA seasons: 30 & 42 goals).

#3 --- *Denis Potvin -------- 185 Goals.

#4 --- *Doug Wilson -------- 55 Goals.

#5 --- Ron Greschner ----- 145 Goals.

#6 --- *Larry Robinson ---- 141 Goals

#7 --- Barry Beck ----------- 103 Goals.

#8 --- Bob Murray ---------- 102 Goals.

#9 --- Randy Carlyle ------- 97 Goals.

#10 -- Brad Maxwell -------- 95 Goals.

#11 -- *Bjore Salming ------ 94 Goals.

#12 -- *Brad Park ----------- 90 Goals. (played only 8 seasons).

#13 -- Robert Picard ------- 86 Goals.

All other Defenseman All-Time

*Hall of Fame.

#7 All-Time Defensemen Most Seasons of 58 or more points-Larson-9 in

12 seasons played, all players higher had more seasons played than Larson most with substantially more seasons played: -#6 with 3 more seasons played; #5 and higher, one had 8 more, three had 9 more, and one had 10 more seasons played. Larson is #2 most seasons of 58 points or more of players in 15 seasons or less played, second only to Denis Potvin, had 10 seasons of 58 points or more in 15 seasons played.

Defense-Number of Seasons of 58 or more points; and Seasons played:

#1 -- 17 seasons - Ray Bourque ----- 22 seasons played:

#2 -- 13 seasons - Paul Coffey ------- 21 seasons played;

#3 -- 11 seasons -- Larry Murphy ---- 21 seasons played;

#4 -- 11-seasons - Phil Housley ----- 21 seasons played;

#5 -- 11 seasons -- Al McInnis -------- 20 seasons played;

#6 -- 10 seasons - Denis Potvin ----- 15 seasons played;

#7 -- 9 seasons -- Reed Larson ---- 12 seasons played;

#8 -- 9 season ---- Nicklas Lidstrom 20 seasons played;

#9 -- 8 seasons --- Larry Robinson -- 20 seasons played;

#10 - 7 seasons --- Bobby Orr -------- 9 seasons played;

#11 - 7seasons ---- Doug Wilson ----- 16 seasons played;

#12 - 7 seasons --- Chris Chelios ---- 26 seasons played;

#13 - 7 Seasons -- Gary Suter -------- 17 seasons played;

#14 - 6 seasons --- Brian Leetch ----- 18 seasons played;

#15 - 6 seasons --- Scott Stevens ---- 22 seasons played;

#16 - 5 seasons --- Brad Park --------- 17 seasons played;

#17 - 5 seasons --- Bjore Salming --- 17 seasons plsyed;

#18 - 5 seasons --- Mark Howe ------- 16 seasons played-NHL-and 6-WHA in 6 seasons;

-- 11 seasons in 22 seasons played.

#19 - 3 seasons --- Guy Lapointe ---- 14 seasons played;

All 19 defensemen above are in the Hockey Hall of Fame except Reed Larson and Gary Suter.

#1 tied for Most Goals-Larson with 27 goals in 1980-81 Season

#1 - Reed Larson --------- 27;

#1 - Ray Bourgue --------- 27;

#1 - Ron Greschner ------ 27;

#2 - Denis Potvin ---------- 20;

#2 - Rob Ramage --------- 20;

#3 - Mark Howe ------------ 19;

#3 - Ian Turbull ------------- 19;

#4 - Paul Reinhart --------- 18;

#4 - John Van Boxmeer -- 18;

#5 - Risto Sittanen -------- 17;

#6 - Larry Murphy --------- 16;

#6 - Randy Carlyle -------- 16

#2 in Most Goals-Larson with 22 goals in 1981-82 Season

#1 - *Mark Howe ----------- 24;

#2 - Reed Larson --------- 22;

#3 - *Bjore Salming ------- 19;

#4 - *Ray Bourque -------- 17;

#5 - *Larry Robinson ----- 14;

31

The hardest shot in hockey took a lot of work, a lot of training, a lot of exercises, a lot of focus and determination, a lot of time on the ice as the foundation for the strength that built this incredible shot of Reed Larson. Larson did all of these things. Larson was known to be one of the strongest players in the game with deep physical strength and he also had strong inner strength shown in how in treated others. Larson had principles that guided his life.

The Reed Larson Principles are a way to live life. All teammates are important, stand up for every teammate; give back to the community to those who need a little help, give back to hockey with clinics, youth hockey, coaching, teaching, and to right the wrongs.

The **Reed Larson Principles** are 7 principles:

• **Work hard.** Always work very hard to get better as Larson did in youth hockey, high school hockey, college hockey, and in the NHL;

• **Stand up.** Stand up for your teammates, every one of them. Stand up for others in society, everyone of them. Larson has done this throughout his life including standing up for his fellow NHL players and concussions.

• **Duty.** A duty to all, to make a better life. A duty to teammates and all that played the game of hockey with the concussion lawsuit, a duty to act.

• **Compete, fiercely.** Play the game fiercely, every game, fight hard to win, give it your all, every day in life. Shoot your shot hard, very hard on goal, on your goals in life, just as Reed Larson shot the hardest shot in hockey putting an explosive force, everything he had into every one of his slap shots. Take the example of Reed Larson and put everything you have got into everything you do.

• **Give back to the community.** Serve others by serving charities and the community.

• **Give back to hockey.** Coach, instruct, and give back to those who played the game.

• **Joyful spirit. Love life and others with a joyful spirit!** Larson has had a high spirit of a "love of life" throughout his journey that connects with everyone along his journey.

Of the game of Hockey, Larson says he, "loved it all", and "it was a blast playing". He was one of the fiercest competitors in the game, one of the leaders of the game, a dominating player who loved the game, Reed Larson has given us a grand example of a way to live life. We can take from the Reed Larson Principles a lesson or two for our own lives in our own style on our journey of life. Onward, with the Reed Larson Principles for a better hockey, a better life for teammates, a better life for those in our lives, a better us in living our lives, and a better life for all.

NOTES:

1. University of Minnesota athletics/hockey website.
2. NHL.com, and WHA.com.
3. HHOF.com/inductee-Hockey Hall of Fame website.
4. NHL.com
5. Ibid.
6. Ibid.
7. Ibid.
8. "Larson launches Wings, 7-3", by Bill McGraw, Detroit Free Press Feb. 16, 1983, page 3-D.
9. Lakepulaski.com
10. NHL.com-lesterpatrickaward.

INDEX: